v v v

Speaks for Itself

A Commodity of Musings

from My Life

v v v

Jeffrey Paul Bailey

v v v

About the Author

Jeffrey is a Worcester, Massachusetts resident and graduate of Assumption College in 1997. He worked for years with and was an avid fan of several underappreciated female recording artists. He's looking to collaborate on custom prose for weddings and other of life's milestones.

https://facebook.com/jeffreypb

https://twitter.com/Esoterrorca

https://instagram.com/bailey9885/

Contents

Snow

Another day to loaf around,
Excuses already delayed,
Your mind's made up anyway.
Such stillness is right outside your window:
the vast expanse which is so close
the horizon inevitably meets this place.
Your shouts are an echo of the past.
You take a breath; we'll see what's left.
Who knows why you're cut off?
Isolation is the cold you chose.
A vision blankets these years -
it could be just as easily now, or any number of years ago:
time unwinds with the newly fallen snow.

Death

Gunfire on the crowded steps of an emporium in this dream;
everyone assumes a lifeless position
presumed dead by all accounts
since this never ends...

Face down, hands down
lifeless as anyone
incapacitated by unerring fear
it could be...

They are playing dead
to save our lives
so many of us have already succumbed or triumphed
and still I have yet to awaken...

to look death in the face.

To The Exclusion of Others

I couldn't help but notice
we are all in the same sinking boat
but it doesn't figure into my escape plan
I feel as though I'm all alone
in the midst of a mayday overblown.

Sink or swim
even if your life doesn't depend on it;
Know in contemplative meditation
with each breath given
each moment which can't be relived
should be the ones to make you insist
that your mind never again fall victim
even if those around you have forgotten and are unwilling.

Teacher's Pet

A compliment is something of a tease;
a sort of lifeline for those who don't believe.

Those words uttered by anyone else
would seem less credible, and I'd be more skeptical
but it's all the more reason I want them to be true
because they came from you -
but I won't be on my knees.

So we all long to be heard -
a subtle nuance from the longing I feel
that has required of me too much in the way of reserve
yet ended somehow in my getting hurt.

I want to make you keep blushing
until your nervous laughter makes you lose composure
and pin you
not only to a commitment
but exchange words through mouths that make understanding
more fluid.

May I always make a willing participant
to my teacher whose discipline
is reserved for his best student.

A Day To Be Free

So I'm not listening to hear "no".
You tell me - in one ear, out the other it goes.
I'm on a mission to break your spell
put in motion a long time ago
into a mind which could not envision
I could beat the odds if I escape your prison.

You'd call me broken
when I had no idea how to fix it
but I had to detach myself from reality;
sometimes those too close insert themselves in our present
as if the future's just a shared investment of the past.
Those who cloud our dreams are those who someday make us
in the face of fear yet love and devotion run free.

Only you can be a distraction
if I acknowledge you, you - yes you.
This song and dance loses its rhythm
and to you my madness has no rhyme.
To some a dream is just too precious
but this life yearning to be someday free
won't be built on a memory
as if it were a keepsake to be looked on fondly.

There's no better connection broken
than the one you lose
when you no longer acquiesce
to all the appeals to reasons and grumbled objections
knowing someday we'll be free and heal those wounds.

Den of Iniquity

In this den of iniquity
these sheets and blankets make up the bed
I'll never lie in;
for others will never see what lies beneath
where the darkness and my passions meet
inside the head.

Almost three decades of pleasure
can't be mistaken for addiction;
when there's no one to enable you
your passion is only as pure
as long as it endures.

There's never been anyone to touch,
Never did I have to worry about the reciprocity of trust.

The faces, the places and the dens of iniquity always change
but the same comforts of home exist never with shame
while to others these simple pleasures seem strange.

No one above or beneath me;
yet I'm living a life aberrant
but with a loving parent
who is in denial I'm no longer in my youth
and before he grows too old
and I fear I'm going to lose both
in this den of iniquity
we can be a family.

Waiting for the Other Shoe to Drop

Here I go again walking out the door
for better or worse, I have to be coerced,
not knowing if I'll walk back to you
or something worse.

Distance between us today cannot be measured in miles or hours,
when past experience mars the faith
that in this window
I'll see you again is shaken forevermore.

Lives in peril;
somehow you repeatedly jettison the recommendations
and attempt to rewrite the prescription
as if health always on the mend
can by upheld by your constitution.

I left you with too much hesitation -
all the while the risk much greater to me
should I choose to stay;
too many times with grace you pulled through
but to defy the odds in advance.
When none of us can predict the future
you're remarkably certain
while you insist I'm acting too prematurely.

She needed your support
but the more you thought you did right by her

the worse it got.
I'm not paralyzed by immobility
but I rely on you the way she did -
for acknowledgement that your promise
can't bear out when the fruit of life
won't let any of us take another bite.

Old Crows

The storm had yet to come inland
but seagulls were already circling
as if grousing each other
they couldn't be heard by the generations below
who had to wrangle with that meddlesome squawking
which the dumb gulls hoped would be interpreted as advice or
warnings-

not gossip from aged crows.

They took their time in the winter to get here,
usually the setting is summer and their presence
though a nuisance can be tolerated
as long as they're not abusive.

As soon as the thunder ignites an estrogen limbo
they have to stir up a windstorm that blows the excrement far and
wide for the intrusive controversy to foment;
the effects of which are on our car windows...

Incontinent old crows, use your car as a bathroom toilet.

Never feed the gulls
or break bread with them;
when out of respect
you are trying to be kind
they will peck their little noses
and attack en masse

but even among one another
when their backs are turned
there always has to be another feeding frenzy
sticking their noses where they don't belong
all the while pretending to get along.

Masquerading as mother hens,
they're taking stock of on whom it's
best to dump
so others can be mired in funk;
until people can't help noticing there's nowhere else for the birds
to go
only to find the gulls turned into really old crows.

Graveyard Shift

Here lies _____
and nothing else was on his epitaph
about the man who walked through life
never showing the right side
oh yes, he could laugh
but people mistook his joy for their fright.

A little different as a child
reduced, cajoled and ridiculed;
In adulthood he should have been part of a world
where he was celebrated not for his eccentricities
but for the manner of his will
that brought him this far
when as a child he thought himself so weak he never could.

He took to his grave
the tales he spun to those closest to him;
the lies were perpetuated by convention life demanded.

He came in as he went out:
aimless, spineless and penniless.
If he spoke, it was never a sob or cry,
more a dog's whimper begging for its demise.

Loyal to a fault
guilt-ridden and gilded
by the shame instilled, he found himself in the middle

until the days were the worst reminder of what should've been
simple.

He sought refuge where a child would
until that place was no longer vacant;
memories penetrated the safe-haven
He had to come out and stand on his own two feet
but was paralyzed by a world of his own making.
God couldn't indulge,
someone who was close had to help him live this fantasy
if he was ever to see sanity.

A disservice was done to him
but in no way was this a crime of immaturity;
for what his years lacked in his identity
he made up for in blind resolve that one day his wildest dreams
would yield fortune - what he wanted, just to be on his own.

Martyrslaughter

Fight the battles as if the war's already done;
the warrior's weapon was his life
knowing he would be reborn into the glow of eternal light.
Ready to be under the gun,
until desirous of his moment in the sun
he got burnt to a crisp by his own admission.
He would rather have been a martyr -
public opinion was that no one would miss him
but he's still the media's fodder.
Judgment in the face of fear,
all that remains foreign is now a void.
In the cradle of civilization destroyed
the faithful should never be mourned.

The World

You don't want me to hide,
to cut myself off,
it's kind of hard
if not impossible
when the one you won't let me seek
is inside myself.

I'm adrift in whatever -
this resigned uncertainty is
all I can do is wait
for whatever comes my way.

Whatever joy is in the moment
whatever enduring pain it doesn't quite mask
I never had a chance
until suddenly a mistake came to pass.

I can't say I've never misspoken,
You say I told a lie.
I just could never breathe life
into a world of ideas
which in their infancy never became words
before they could be properly formed
much less heard.

I was quarantined in a glass house
just a stone's throw away from the world
so it was able to keep me at bay.

Gaining ground on truth
all the while losing touch
with the rest
of the universe...

To think I would ever know my place in the world...
how absurd.

The Earth is a vacuum consuming and
dense - ready to burst
from the world of hurt.

Machine Madness

Machines became a curse;
We lost the finesse to speak truth gently
to speak without being terse;
too far past the point to have forgone a false sense of security
for there to remain anything but numbing adversity.

In an age of an apocalyptic abyss
it does mankind no greater disservice
when we choose not to be seen
just heard.

Sadly we've lost the ability to read the nuance between rage and
hurt,
any one of us could be the agent or the victim of doom.

Still with all these machines
we're not saved from the ruination
that makes us vulnerable to the regime
that makes the world advance in the face of destruction
with no second chance.

Before It Gets Too Late

Too many times I've not been straightforward
so I'm no longer afraid of persecution

I just want a reward -
To some that would be prostitution.

Tonight I hope I sleep tight
with or without you
but never to know
what I've only dreamed of
before I age out
and it gets too late...

It keeps me up at night, contemplating
way past the point of usefulness...

and it's already too late.

Afraid of the Dark

To be afraid of the dark,
I'm grappling senselessly with the unknown
because we're all alone.

Lay your head down on a pillow reluctantly,
misgivings play tricks when you're
somewhere between a memory
and drifting off to unconsciousness.

The past is just as palpable
embedded in the present.
When you're afraid of the dark
the days grow longer with the weary despair.

Instead of conquering fear
we look over our shoulders
waiting for a judge and jury to appear.
When we should be carefree,
for only what is not meant to be clear
should no longer hold us back;
regretting choices will only
make us rehash them in nightmares.

We are bolder for the absence of light.
We are stars colliding not by some celestial accident
but for once in our lives, by our own right.

Damper

Roll off your shoulder
in one ear and out the other;
You never seem to do as they ask
but they never seem to want to shut their yaps.

Of all the things to criticize
the sweat on your back
seems to indicate his good intentions are a disguise.

While you're supposed to bite your tongue
as he insinuates you look like a worn out dishrag
and your hygiene is compromised...

You feel even dirtier inside.

He should be more preoccupied
by the real problems plaguing this kingdom
than to wonder whether
you're wearing a T-Shirt to sop up what he told you
 was an anatomical error.

Truth is a trifle
as you never use a towel
after a scalding hot shower
when you're in a hurry to a new day
which we won't let him put a damper on.

Get Me Through

It's not so lonely at the top
when everyone's trying to nudge you
from your spot.

Repeat and relax, and say after me
You know there's somewhere else you'd rather be.

You can bury your head in the sand
but the naysayers can still nip and bite your heels;
even while the haters try to tear
the foundation I laid
it all won't crumble in the face of a nefarious plan.

Fighting to hold onto something uniquely yours
is always in vain;
when the work is never done
praise goes unsung,
just the facts, the story of the triumphant one.

Even when you see me dip below
and sink to new lows,
just because you've been in hell longer
I'm not down for the count -
I know no other way to rise above
than with my nose to the sky.
You'll mistake my resilience as indifference
making me all the more certain
that keeping my head held high will get me through.

To Be You

To be you,
without social censure.
What would it take to be you,
to not let them hold you responsible
for the visceral reaction of your own nature,
to just be you.

To be you -
can't have it both ways;
when you have to make choices
you open the floodgates
to all that awaits.

To be you, they'll call these mistakes
and make you even less you.
You'll reinvent
yourself to get ahead,
yet when you're not trying to be yourself
we can all see through
to the authentic proof
so there could never be another you.

Out of Whack

You've always had only one
I guess one
needs to be supplanted by another...

I yearned to feel
(even if I never could again)
What I looked like
Before I looked at you

Before the expanse
Of what I did to myself
Withstanding the insistence, all faculties
were all cylinders ablaze,
but I continued to graze

Till one day...
I couldn't fit into these shirt and pants.

Just because I'm already buried
By gross negligence
And look like shit
The ultimate judgment was mine.

I relied on others to worry,
meanwhile I'm blind
I can't pretend to lose sight
Of all that is
Out of whack.

Guilt

Some things we can't learn;
If only to speak with ease
so all of a sudden in a time of need
our concern could have measure in words
I know your reception to them could albeit lead
to something worse
but when there's never the right thing to say
the pain you feel is our mutual curse
because for this reversal of fortune
neither of us could rehearse.

Now only do I see
how much easier it would have been
if only the distance I should have traversed
was more than halfway
to where you were.

I don't know how walls get built
but what's tearing me down is that you are standing against them.
The habits we've developed have led me to absolve myself
of any guilt.

As if it could get any worse,
but I know it could.

Glass House

You think I am naive enough to believe
I'm the only one with problems.

Maybe that's why -unlike you-
I choose not to dispense advice
as if it were worth more than two cents
the precious little
you have to offer,
I see right through.

Maybe before you closed the door of your glass home
you should have thought twice -
remember I was the one to cast the first stone.

Since you no longer shoulder my burden
Whatever you thought you had to offer
 which you deluded yourself into believing
was working
will let you take pride in my knowing,
in my watching what you now build with sheer delight.

Do us all a favor
save your finest for when you part from the world;
on your deathbed no-one will want to suffer you
while you draw your last breath
trying desperately not to choke on your own words.

Relocate Underground

There are many ways to get underground
but no one's found a way out
once immersed in the darkness.

If connections withstood the passage of time in the light
they're still with me,
even if I'm not standing down
they're still on my mind -
still following me around.

Some may have pushed me asunder -
made me flee to the underground
to retreat deny escape
or find the strength
to stay alive.

I've sentenced myself to this world
neither for the better or for the worse.
There are no choices in limbo -
and ergo no regrets.
Even the hand of fate which I once couldn't defy
can't conspire against me with the broken hand of time.

They urge me to turn toward light and opportunity.
For what was already out of my hands
they demand you take responsibility.

The shame others would cast on me in my despair
could've been my eulogy written prematurely
but no one again will make a fool of me.

Once I go underground
as Jesus dies in vain
only to be resurrected again
there are no more crosses to bear
no more pain
and no more of feelings to spare.

Maybe someday if you consider relocating underground
you will take a second look and decide it's not for you
but any reservations you have already guaranteed
you can't cancel
just because you misunderstood.

Beyond the Love

I've always wanted to know
where the feelings go
If you'd never disappeared
would I have ever realized
this was just an infatuation
beyond the love I thought we made?

The thing about being burned
is the one with scars
earns the right to lay blame for all their days
even at the feet of those whose intention is to make it better
promising never to inflict pain.

They're the rebound scapegoats beyond the love
that could have been made
but I played it safe.

Never moving forward
never letting you in
maybe without years of practice
I can never know the meaning of the word.

So I conjure up the madness
and you the object of wanton affection
find my overtures looking beyond the love
too awkward to even shower me with pity
which I don't want mistaken for compassion.

Love's Ravage

What we will put ourselves through
only not to the extremes
some randoms went to
to rule out these lovers for you
before you even meet...

until the unrealized dreams of those scorned
prompted them to be sent to you.

Love's ravage:
it consumes whatever feelings we have left;
if immune to love
we face a worse affliction...

We're unknowing carriers of a history uncertain
we're all bound to it by a lack of attrition
somehow convincing ourselves we shouldn't have to settle for
anything but the best...

Perfection.

Love's ravage consumes
but when we have no feelings
that makes us inured
so those of us most savage are the ones among us
least fazed by our lovers being so enamored
we take leave of them.
so we have to take leave of them.

I Hope and Wonder

Not sure what's come over me
and for no good reason
the sadness in these eyes
can't bear the highlight of this moment
and they without my say-so make me want to cry.

Maybe reality has finally sunk in...

I thought the worst of it was over
after having borne witness to it,
I thought I'd already exorcised the pain.

I wonder how it all feels
but I guess it's a moot point
since you were always so stoic.

I wonder if you ran
because you were scared
and didn't want to know the plan
or if you were as surprised and wounded
that the God you revered
had one final command.

Some of your words were all too prophetic
The Black Irish in you spoke to your will
that once signed, sealed and delivered
was so punctual as you always were it was cruel.

I hope there's rest now...
even through those nights I heard you tossing and turning in that
lonely room
brought you so little in this life that by unhappiness you were
consumed.

I just hope you find the peace you sought
so you can be at ease
while for an eternity you sleep.

Suspicion/Extinction

Life's a system of a disease underestimated.
Those who breathe this air
giving and getting more
shouldn't have procreated.

By all accounts there has been epic failure;
now we're on the verge of extinction
when we're too suspicious
of our own futures unwritten.

We came together to unearth a breed of underclass
once only preserved by a furtive history
and by those that would segregate
the different kinds of human trash.

Those that never would hold themselves in judgment
with suspicion cast an awkward glance
at the man with hair down to his rear-end
but that could just as easily be some pour soul's only friend.

Just as those about whom I talk smack
or the ones smoking crack
or just wearing clothes too far down past their *ss-cracks
it takes all kinds to bring a civilization under attack.

He who thinks his own don't stink
must be more frightened when he sees

an unwelcome co-mingling that breeds
for soon his own species will be extinct.

Be There (Despair)

Never a word uttered
but you can merrily self-destruct;
wanting me to live in your denial
but now all I want to do is run.

Yet at the same time you think you are helping us come to terms
by keeping me
under your thumb...

You became housebound;
it can't be that challenging if you don't try
now your drawn-out unshaven face and forlorn eyes
they signify your imminent passage from this life
resigned to what comes next
even before it's time.

Still you want the best for me
while I watch you admit
you're panicked I won't be there...

to watch you withdraw only feeds into your despair.

It's kind of hard to be of more help to you
let alone myself
when the outstretched arms that reach out all at once are unaware
of the depths to which you've sunk
and your fear
of what's to come

rational or not
is a silent battle that can never be won.

You Want Me To Stop

You want me to stop because
someone else does.
You think I have a problem;
you were the first to hit rock-bottom.
You've wallowed in self-pity
through indulgences of years
and you want me to turn back the clock
for both of us.

You're a bundle of nerves;
an engine running on fear
about what I'll become
when you're no longer here.

So you want me to stop just because
you pinned all that on me
and you want me to stop because
the apple does not fall far from the tree.

When your view of your own life grew maudlin
I could've been on my last leg hobbling
but sowing those seeds of wild oats
when you could no longer
stand on our own...

it only made me stand my ground.

I should've done it long ago
but when your growth is stunted
you have a lot of time to make up for.
You want me to stop just because after all these years
you feel my example is improper.

Like clockwork, you know what makes me tick
because life is like dawn
up until the ring of the last-call,
I'm not stopping because
You know I want to have fun.

Stunted Growth

I'm looking for more than a coping mechanism.
All the years of pain walking the path of least resistance
I was still reveling in the pestilence of shame.

Where most people see a challenge
where most people find reward in growth -
I fought whatever came my way.

Would that I be reborn and baptized in the same water
that showed favor and flowed
to those whom I loathe,
taken with a grain of salt it was status-quo.

So unfazed by let-down after let-down
even when missteps were past permissible,
inured to defeat
I let myself stumble
and without a second thought
with no one to give me the benefit of the doubt
all alone I stuck it out.

I get back on my feet
for another journey that ends
the way they all end
but in all this
the same lesson, never learned

is the one once more
I'm supposed to repeat.

It's almost as if the mystery is solved
but the reasoning I'll never discern
just because you want me to understand out of concern.

Dreams (Would That One Day)

Yet again I woke up today to no surprises
but no sense of purpose

in my life.

I can remember when
the wonder of my adolescence
warmed by the shed
of morning sun
and by spring's early light
made the opportunities seem
endless.

When the days appeared to have no consequence
that was all the more reason to relish life as if it were
still those same mornings repeating
and the dreams were so vivid in real-time
that I longed for the world at my feet
and that dreams could carry me through
a chosen yearning of sleepless nights.

Would that that dreaming
would finally lend me the muse
to forge my own path
where I could shine so brightly under the moon;
using the little with which I was imbued

still not fall prey to the rampant indifference
which programmed me to accept their abuse.

Would that one day I could win with the germ of imagination;
that one of those planted seeds that were tossed and blowing in
the wind
make me free and towering
to realize every unfulfilled need.

Leash (Emasculate)

Strings and whips have more give
but to you recreation is only for winning.
If you wrap me around your finger
for a mere moment
I hate to inform you
but you can't celebrate
when you have me dangling by a thread.

I'm ready to bolt over something you said.

You deny love as if you were afraid
you'd given me too much
and you wouldn't get enough.
I shouldn't be rewarded
by begging for your touch.

You shouldn't tie a leash on me
when I can't turn around in all my uncertainty
with a cone of shame around my neck and see
all your deceit.

You're really the old ball and chain;
I'm for someone who deserves the one that got away.

but when I found a new home
I thought to belong was to be loved.

With my unspoken loyalty
with that leash you trained me
in no uncertain terms
by command you schooled me
to listen and not to be heard.

You'd pull that leash way too tight
as if it were to choke my neck
where no one could identify
any baubles or tags with my name
to show I was kept.

Regime

There's really no shelter
when you can't be sure of your safety;
acclimating to one extreme
when natural daylight can even poison you with its rays, but
to be isolationist may mean to be led astray
when everything's a multitude of colors cloistered in world of
black, white and gray.

The world may turn on a dime
but it's not always dark before it's time to say goodbye.

Maybe the refuge we seek isn't in the answers they speak
so in the meantime we refuse to face the clock's last stand
so nothing or no one is such an imposition as to be definite.

Someone with power to conquer your fears
will make quite a steal;
he who does this could govern
with visceral appeal.

Anarchy riots of the imagination
if only could make palatable...
the crazed empire's downfall
that can't even sustain a border wall...

otherwise the future of mankind will be compromised
because objective reality will be marginalized.

Mechanized gesticulations
Pavlovian expectations
there's no shock and awe;
gone is the element of surprise.
Only the most suspicious ire will be raised
while the atrocities reign against the media's reality show refrain.

Somehow only random acts of kindness
will be televised to the American-turned-Stepford husband's
wives;
Big Brother's hypocrisy only not in color, but in black and white
while the victimization heightened by the urgency
of some insurgency against too many enemies
while the commercials pull at the heartstrings of those with
feelings...

all the while we live in fear of our misgivings.

Silence by Proxy

You abandoned
all semblance
Of the life we had.
You apparently didn't have to go
As far as I
to lie to yourself
That you weren't guilty for
what it was
you inevitably would become.

It feels as if I've been
Running away aimlessly
for the two of us;
All the anger that covered fear,
all the times we felt smaller through the years.

I didn't think you would let me bare
the guilt if we're supposed to heal.

You're older and still running
And for as long as my memory serves
I've been subsisting on false hope
That my best dreams will reimburse...

A prelude to a warning...

Now there are too many
Causes for concern

It's funny what we reveal when
We're dodging each other's messages;
Evading the overtures
By the proxy of silence

The sterility of reservation...

I don't want to run
until I can't
because it hurts.

Transference

Obsessed with so many faces..

Those who shine brightest
give me the alternate reality.
I can brandish a promising imagination.

Even if to you
I pose
sight unseen
You think you're just one of many
And I take the focus off me

and put it on someone I've never met
Who takes up permanent residence
in a penthouse in my head.

I have something to offer.
You've never met me
But I still think
you're my raison d'être.

Not to feel
not to believe
Nor know me...

Yet there still only need be one you.

Too much of me
all it took
was only one misstep
to lead to subsequent catastrophes.

Standing in the shadows is a shame
But too much time spent afraid
Castes a maudlin refrain

I've no wonder
No valor

Maybe the light
Could have shined longer;
You and all the others
could have regaled me for
what is so profitable
In your vanity and fame.

Pursued

The impulse is its own reward
For a desire so untoward
Should I walk away
Should I just be so bold
Either way
You won't give me what you sold

The power of suggestion
I'm clear on what was said
Nothing as mundane as the literal
Should require me
To hazard a guess
When this bliss
outweighs the risk

Words lie in the interpretation
I haven't a question
So if this is a tease
I admire your subtlety
In the way you can't
Admit
You want me.

Sweet Spot

Just with anything in life
it takes time to hit your stride
but when it's right
it's that sweet spot you like.

You'll wonder your whole life
maybe asking why
and then you'll die
when you should have just given in
not certain if there's a hell
not certain if there's a heaven
just to save yourself from who knows what
while unconscious in your burial plot -
not a known sweet spot.

To the arbiters of virtue, to those who would have us chaste
for those dying to live
there's no shame
in my sweet spot that remains.

I get pleasure in knowing your center
gets us to desire's core...

and the hotter it gets
it leaves me wanting more...

How you could have made vows
to prophets, deities and priests

and apparitions far and wide
seems all too ill-advised
when now your sweet spot wows
and gets me there every time...

even if it leads to our demise.

Oceans

If ever the front passes through
with its winds of promises to cool things off
never will I be so subtle
as to go unnoticed
when I blow past you...

Down-under hemisphere
where the tides are reversed
love can bloom in our Fall's Spring
and we didn't have to be any the wiser
or left with doubt to our own devices
because the winter's neutralized when nothing dies.

This is a time and space
unknown to you and me
devoid of hesitation of fear...

It took oceans of infinite depth
-an underwater precipice-
to take this plunge without prejudice.

I couldn't fathom what it took
to hit rock-bottom
until you deemed this is a lapse in judgment
when you decided
we deviated too far off course.

You steered us to some distant shore
without life-vests
only to find my heart broken instead of a treasure chest.

A cave, an abyss in your ocean
dares the faint of heart
to take a risk
to believe you can feel loved
but not to know the deepest leagues of devotion.

Lost Youth

Contemplating what's led me down this road
I didn't know I was on course
to settle for less...
as the fights grew more and more intense.

Every ending opened a trap door
to one more room with the walls caving in
it shattered my optimism
that I could get from under of my own thoughts
and out on my own...

There's little comfort in knowing
you're where you're supposed to be.

Even if there's a light at the end of the tunnel
when you've been in the dark so long
the specter of what might be on the other side
is a panoramic view through myopic eyes...

You long for everything to be black and white.

No one bargains to come into this world of objective truth;
for someone to tell us what to do
when all of our own accumulated experiences are prohibitive.

Head in the Clouds

Every image of my life:
fist-cuffed behind my back.

Arrested by circumstances;
always handicapped by the undoing of my past.

A growth stunted
by lashing out;
ashamed of a string of mistakes
led by my selfish world view
that seemed to become
a string of ineptitude.

It's a waste when one so smart
can't sustain enough discipline to embrace
what it is he needs to admit are his weaknesses
and find his inner strengths.

My calling eluded me
but even to stay grounded is still a tall order;
without footing or a direction
for even the most practical of agendas.

My head stays in the clouds;
the nearest edifice to heaven
where my head's been full of high-minded
but possibly misguided intentions.

Prone to Fall

Born to crawl
only once a miracle
elevated us...

to pick ourselves up and walk.

If only by these bootstraps
these harnesses that buckle us...
when we jump with eagle eyes
we could fly for dear life.

In a world where there would be reverence
for heights scaled
we would still thrive
soaring on our laurels
and complacency wouldn't be a vice
but an enduring promise to all...

We'd never be prone to fall.

Aspirations so unrealized they were never defined;
situations arise remedied by new design,

Evolution by necessity led us through detours;
flying by the seat of our pants all these years.

Applauded for being willful, obsession becomes ritual.

So the unforeseen destination
could never fulfill when it propelled my anger
when my bitterness was my only weapon.

I shut out the external and reached the pinnacle of no return.

We may be born to crawl
but only being human
made me prone to fall.

Neighbor

You had to confirm
what your prying mind
thought it had already known.
So when I didn't care I may offend you
You had the audacity to wonder why
I didn't feel ashamed by your reproach.

Rooted in denial of what I couldn't let go
I told you no when clearly the answer was yes -
what I couldn't resist.

One-sided erotic wanton fantasy;
you in the adjoining split to my left
and I in my Colonial
I turned twelve
when I succumbed to my thoughts
not knowing I needed anyone to stimulate me
as much as my own sex.

When you said hello
when you were out plowing your lawn
I imagined you were playing coy with your smile
your shirt was already off
and since our last encounter I made you cop
to your own uncertainty.

Neighbor, neighbor
I see you and me through the reflection of my bedroom window
Neighbor, neighbor
You've moved round my way
Neighbor, neighbor
come up to my room and play
Neighbor, neighbor
Till then I'll be bumping my rug thinking of you
as lust, not always for you, compels me to do.

Fated

Saddle up to anyone
who'll give a free ride
I had to be desperate for something more
to be so blind.

While we gallivanted through
the freedom of nights in our youth
we never stopped to think how we would overcome
our insecurities
to be of use.

When it came time to face the music
and realize we did nothing for each other
but inflict abuse
I could've stood alone but never would.

On that fateful day I had my door ajar
the goal was to meet uplifting people
with whom someday I could relate
as they were quietly going about their own business
and working towards an end game
but through a mutual acquaintance there you stood
and the parental advisory to meet as many people as I could
couldn't have been a more undesired destiny
as if my prayers not only went unfulfilled
but were never heard.

No Love Lost

Haven't seen you in your latest incarnation;
seems as if it's been beyond ages
since we've spoken
but your words buckled under the pressure
you always felt I put on you
when I would dare express
my displeasure.

I guess I had an expectation some things could be different
but the bar can't be set any higher
when your moral compass abandoned me
and what I knew of you
back when
you used to be
even if in name only
some semblance of my mother.

You said you needed to evolve.
You saw nothing changing
and as your illness progressed
you were the tight harness on our family
putting our will to bear it to the test.
Your last act was as though it were a death.

Even if you don't know, you're complicit
in your own theft.

Somehow you lost touch with us;
if I ever thought in our mutual delusion
I could reach you
now to think love is a lost pursuit
when your tears once fertilized a young soul
and your compassion
was once a blessing
my memories of you have left me numb from the cold.

Mama Said Make Friends

I wish I could go back and place
where I went wrong
or if I were too young
or too obtuse
to ever nuance
who if anyone would
come into my life
and make the amount of my history
add up
to something right
if I weren't of sound mind.

I kept the door open to all possibility.
I should have shut out selectively
all personality
in whose clenched desperation
my tolerance stretched beyond
what I envisioned for companionship.

Too easily led by the nose
My inertia let them know
I could accept the status-quo
and that I'd be content living alone
yet they were all too content
I had nowhere to go.

I chose to live vicariously through those
whose companionship I took for a
rodeo show.

Never discerning
the respect ultimately I should command
was my own.

Artificial Faith

Moving forward requires a lobotomy
If we are the sum of our experiences

Shouldn't this moment be mindful
of the steady composure that grounded me
of the blind faith that yielded virtue?
if God tries to save us

I will never err if I believe and act on my behalf
I will never look back to you wondering what I could've had
I'm merely an afterthought plagued at different times for
unverifiable absolution
For sins
past, present
or future.
Your church at best provides me shameless fleeting camaraderie
In the midst of life's hypocrisy.

The Luxury of Complacency

I toy with ideas like I play with myself.
It's all so hypothetical
the possibilities are endless.
When you're not a risk taker
everything you contemplate
seems dangerous.
I'm afraid I won't ever realize
What it was I was supposed to be
even when the moment comes
I'll play dumb.
Somehow I thought endings freed
but the possibilities of possibility
overwhelm me.
A life built on dreams
is as paralyzing
as it always seemed.
Stability is a crutch we can't live without
Until it's taken away.
The harsh truth is
that there really is no crutch: you have no leg to stand on.

Fun to Be Loved

Fun to be loved
only never to be won;
fun to be loved
only never to have begun.

These days are a passion play
vying for thrills superficial.
My ego is no more assured
than my will.

In the best case scenario
the object of affection is merely that
never wanting more than
a wanton Lothario.

The love that you feel
made you too vulnerable
to me
for it had to reveal
We have to part ways
not just with each other
but with an ideal.

Self-preservation
from a true awakening
Yet with every day in your absence, with every breath

I have to hold onto life, dear life
with no authority left.

Fun to be loved
only never to have won;
Fun to be loved
only never to have begun.

No one can know love
other than only to feel it;
To know it will never be requited
only to have your heart
slighted.

The Role of Scapegoat

His pseudo-positivism fell on deaf ears
while the others more genuine
have greater reason to be threatened
as his seeds of deception
bear no fruits to reap.

I tuned him out long ago
not willing to buy the dime-store clichés.
The '80s were the age of self-help
(too bad it keeps taking him so long)
but it wouldn't matter if
he'd always be able to put himself first
but his borrowed platitudes don't apply
when everyone else is on the front lines.

For as long as possible I stayed under the radar
one day I'll be unable to escape
the trigger-happy cross-hairs;
the projection of anger through an eagle-eyed glare.

Those who stayed remained quiet,
complacent if only by the fog
of their own resignation
To the misguided but guardedly optimistic notion
that once the reign of militant mischief
was lifted
things could be different.

I too fell in line with stagnation
something was in the air
but it wouldn't abate.

While the other minions would ruminate
even before his sneaky exodus
the man who ran the asylum
checked out prematurely blabbering the rhetoric
with the same hysteria
with which one would yell fire
in a burning edifice.

Instead of looking inward
he put the onus on everyone else's shoulders
as if to manage is only to delegate
with an iron fist
until finally there were only old glories in his favor he couldn't
twist.

He couldn't rest on his laurels
and the shortcomings came oozing through
and despite convictions to the contrary
somehow those successes once attributed to me
were overshadowed by the brass pointing fingers at him
and the roles were suddenly reversed;
to think all along this was rehearsed.

He was spineless under the weight of his own words:
live by the sword, die by the sword.

I gave blood, sweat and tears
only to be told I was insubordinate.
Someone's always to blame;
it's always your fault
when a hierarchy doesn't know or care
how blame is appropriated
as long as a cleaner house somehow convinces them
you were the bad seed eliminated.

The stage is set for them to point fingers at you
and the unsung heroes take the fall.

You've been a scapegoat all along.

Pompous Circumstance

Come hell or high water
or maybe something in between
less extreme
mark my words
for they will resonate
with all those who thought they could seal my fate
and turn around
then label me as a reprobate;

once the wrongs are righted there will be no complaints.

I've traveled many paths
into darkness
I didn't need the agents of promise to get me started.

Maybe the coaches
- all of whom were false prophets -
could fess up to their own incompetence.

Accused me of thinking I was superior;
never did such flattering words get uttered
from those so insincere
I had to question it before
I accepted it as a truth too hard to conceal;
for if it were supposedly a compliment
in my times with them peaceful yet repressed
then surely in the heat of the moment
when passions ignited new threats
it had to be time for them to confess.

Deaf, Dumb, and Blind

Paying lip-service to the attendant victims
as if this were a slaughter to the war;
their motivation is propaganda
to the innocent bystander;

except this is not a battlefield.

You know you've already won.
You prop up the ones who'll get hurt.
You seem to get off at work.

Underestimated
Two-faced is too plain a description;
you shed skin each time you lie
truth to you is like a zebra changing its stripes
you lie like a chameleon changes its color
so you can hide;
it should be a sin to make the blind faithful
wonder.

When your crimes haven't yet been realized
and the jurisdiction is your own mind
everyone will be the scapegoat for devoting their blood, sweat and
time
to a cause that which goes against
their own best interests
and that even your publicly disgraced mind
can no longer rationalize.

When there's nothing to gain
and you've bled everything out of them
they're indignant because like manna from heaven
it dawned on them
your words are trite...

as if to you the one spewing them non-stop
this should come as a surprise.

Over and over...

until the ones who were well-mannered
(meaning silent)
revolt against the tide
and can no longer turn a blind eye.

Your pseudo-positivism should have fallen on more than the deaf
ear
but the visionaries within your circle perpetuated your myth
through the manipulation of your Word
as only false prophets could.

The more genuine among them
stood together spreading a message they gleaned from common
sense
to see they have reason to be threatened
as your seeds of deception
would reap no fruits
while vapidly you stood.

My Bliss

Take refuge in my fantasy;
the space is endless
yours to visit regardless
of our reality.

It might not be what you had in mind
but it's a pleasant excursion
in your head or mine
We can easily get there anytime.

That feeling of déjà vu -
If only the dreams could reveal to us
why we will do inevitably what we do;
the moment it comes
I'm not baffled by what lead to this
Actualized, realized -
either way this is bliss.

Never Go Back

You can't burn bridges
when on either side
there's nothing left to salvage.

It's driven me past the point of blind faith
and I've never come back from that agitated state
only to an awakened hate
I'd rather forget
like a self-induced coma
it wasn't what the doctor ordered.

Never go back
when it was they who led me astray.
I'm right on target
an arrow made for this flight
not to be intercepted by their lies
I'll still hit the bulls-eye.

So there's no going back
when you're on point
so close to the threshold
of a fortune and bliss I wholly control.

I'll never go back
over what I did or said
it was just for a moment

and my life's but the bat of an eye
I shouldn't have to justify.

I'm still in some deity's hands
but I'll never be under their command;
when what all that awaits from them are the decrees
of shame, pain and regret
all of which should have led to my salvation yet.

Never go back to the well
for abuse
to make another wish come true
when I have to live here in spite of all of you.

You'll Never Know (Modesty and

Arrogance)

You'll never know
who cares about you
when you're exiled from
the castle you thought
too sound
for them to penetrate
the walls.

They will be there
to orchestrate your undoing
or want to pick you up
when you come down.

You'll never know
because you're the only one
walking this road
alone...

Pride will force you
to dismiss them all
and keep your head higher
never acknowledging
a downfall...

They can build you up
before or after
you've surrendered your power;
either way it makes no difference
your beliefs are your only hubris.

That which doesn't kill us makes us stronger.
Shot down so many times before
it feels as though
a series of encounters with death
have established
a patterned choke-hold.

So someday I may yet learn
to be the Savior reborn...

but you'll never know.

Passing Glance

Tonight while alone
I had a moment to reflect
back on your words
in lieu of you
a bevy of thoughts...

I can't conquer your heart.

You can just as readily give it to someone else.
I don't know if I was fortunate
you spared me.

You don't see me doing anything
apart from you.
I'm in the darkness with you
and yet we couldn't be more apart;
in the light
an idealized version of you
time to think about some world
where I'm in your view.

The magnetism of fate
or is it the other way around?
Within what I knew as the confines of these halls
a door was opened
not because you wanted it to
but I couldn't stay away

and I'd like to think neither could you
that it wasn't just a phase
or a passing glance...

Stares

Only to know why we're so resistant;
if only I could give into a wish
that twinkle in your eye
and give in to the feelings unrequited.

The looks were playful at first.
I felt the chemistry
almost as though we were children.
At first you felt something too but acted casually
as if it hurt.

Always on your terms
I felt honored
but wondered if there would be a time
We couldn't be alone
face-to-face
without the future being already known.

My fears were allayed
every time we looked in each other's eyes
and during the pauses in conversation
I felt we had built up each other's egos
not just a rapport
but so much that a new form of foreplay
had come to be.

If we could just get past those blank stares,
still somehow you wanted to keep flying
under the radar.
You would have me believe there was
no depth to what we shared
to justify my broaching the subject
of what comes next.

If only you could come with me
to our last frontier...
We would have shown them
with all their reservations
all those vacant stares weren't for not;
once ours in denial, now our faces chiseled eternally
in a kiss...

I still can look into your eyes
and you're not far behind.
The times put a wrap on us,
so unfair our stolen moments
are memorialized by those stares
that to this day to say that we lost touch
makes me blush.

Tomorrow Mourning

These morets are impositions;
even behind closed doors
some stranger's prying eyes of disapproval
urge you to feel shame
whichever way you choose to play.

Are you ashamed of your body?
I'd advise you to grow a thicker skin.
The motive of lust is a sin;
it gives you just cause
to be proud to indulge and give in.

Last night was a means to an end...
The dawn of a new day
it dictates that it's possible to buy absolution;
religion is the common currency
before you're dead
amid all this hypocrisy.

In the meantime and for the happily-ever-after
goodwill towards mankind
is a karmic ideal
you choose to strive for again.

The Worst Force

Just to feel secure
as your bloodshed turns to fruit
all that they ask for in return...
is you.
Death and need are realities one-in-the-same
you can never make the ends meet;
you never know when.
All that which never even had a chance
to pass you by
inevitably keeps moving farther away;
you think your biding your time
you're merely wishing away the days.
Life is hunger as it passes
you'll starve anyway.

Year '93: Denial Foretold

I'll blaze a trail
in your honor
say your name like an Om over and over
till you'd respond I'm going to blow
my own cover
from the box, handicapped
by our thoughts...

Think of you
You're somehow there
Think of you
maybe more than you care.

I merely uttered your name
and daylight vanished
but the path we were on remained...

No warmth, no cold
Am I getting warmer or getting colder?

No closer to what I saw
but couldn't touch;
after all these years
a shadow after which
I lust
even you still insist
you saw me first.

If This is Home

If this is home
it's a mildly pleasant feeling to be back
since I gather I've never know
I've only been
all alone.

If this is home
surrounding me are the things
they say no one can live without
that should be all I need
that should be all it takes
I'm no different from anyone else
one would think.

I smell my mother on me
I emerged clean and pure
and it brought back
how little it took for her
to comfort me
to desert me
all mere memories -
precious they may be
yet to be anything other than something
not able to revoke my pride
for me to look too far into the past
not to see the light.

If this is home
I'm developing paranoia
I like to call it my sixth sense
for things I couldn't repress
but rather forget...

Never since picked up the phone;
the immediacy
the urgency of a message
which became a fortune
from which I've yet to learn.

Impose

You'll impose your will
until you're put in check.
I can't find a way to tell you tactfully
as your friend to accept
to live and let me live
and not with your own agenda
project your own insecurities
hustling, dispensing advice...

This investment of time
could be better spent on your life
rather than on mine.

A dogmatic intrusion sabotaged
what I thought were the best of intentions.

When you felt deceived
by the same token
I thought your words were of genuine concern
so I lied just to humor you
but when it's about my own life
I don't owe you
any truth.

Given your own issues
what you were trying so forcefully to impose
under a black cloud of warnings and doom
only made it clear the bubble
had to let me out
so I could make it burst.

Worldwide Lobotomy

You're looking for a new start
where you can be out of yourself;
unfortunately it won't work
to venture very far.

You possess the shame;
carry baggage as if it were extraneous cargo...

Still it's got to go...

on its maiden voyage
each time never reaching the port of call
sunk by freight to the bowels of hell.

Maybe you shouldn't stray
unless you're certain the destination
reaps rewards
but without that sense of adventure
and appreciation
of the promises of the unknown
you can never let go.

Somewhere not far from home
dawn climbs over a restless night
yielding to a day where the mind has autonomy -
where your alarm call
is the worldwide lobotomy.

If there's to be any peace
there must be peace-of-mind.
No point in giving you a piece of mine -
through the worldwide lobotomy
we'll be fine.

Extricate

Alone time-
no one but me
nothing exciting;
just needed an option
for a little reprieve
from you
while I wasn't doing the straight and narrow
like the way you always think I need to.

Didn't need any alcohol
to escape our mutual withdrawal;
didn't need to hear you
to feel your disapproval.

The greatest of my inhibitions
I suppressed lest I regress
so I channeled all your noise
into non-productive nonsense.

If I told you everything
there would be nothing left
since I have nothing to show
when I haven't grown
and maybe admitting the truth
would provoke the revolution I need
and the awakening you wanted for me.

Eternal adolescence -
waiting naively for the stage
when I can break from our silence
when the world was supposed to be full of promise.

How Long A Hero

I'm pleading to be the one
who's sought after for wisdom;
even after my shameless campaigns
I've never been anyone's number one.

I guess that made me the victim...

How long can a hero
get's a hero's refrain;
How long can I be on a pedestal
when the energy to maintain hero status
zaps me into rashness?

How long can a hero fly in the face of madness
before it make him want to crawl and hide?

How long can a hero last
when the entrapment of the web of success
leads him to places even a hero's mind can't survive?

How long can I be a hero
when without being grounded
to withstand the notion of humility
the hero would rather fall
than have to climb and scrape his way back into your favor
forgoing all modesty?

By the Dark of Night

Full-on get your freak on
Dipped and double-dipped to get a rise.
The dark dumps the weight of inhibitions
One-hundred percent satisfaction knows no compromise.

Strangers from dusk to dawn;
never by the light of day can we make it work
or could an unrelenting imagination be satiated.

The gambit runs from the top to the bottom.
Kisses that were on stand-by ignite the night.
The lovelorn feast prods and pokes
as if the tease were supposed to be enough.

Before chartered territory can be uncovered
hot and bothered would get me a killing cold shower
flowin', flowin'
You reign over me.
Your interest that never wanes,
the humidity will never drop long enough for me to stop.

Just as I'm galvanized by your body's elasticity
I'm nonetheless flexible to your touch;
malleable to the condition -
whatever your command
I wish for so much.

In and Out of Consciousness

When real life floods into nightmare
your life's vision is impaired.
In the repository of the mind
the next day should be clear.

I'm not saying I have to have sweet dreams
because they never come true.
I'm just saying I'd prefer a respite
from a subconscious mind
that clearly can't shake loose
all that should be left behind.

Watch me muddle through regret;
asleep with my life in rewind.
Tonight -
I'm a spectator to my own life
in objective black and white.

Yet dreaming is a mere device
all of it converges to the faces
of those party to my mistakes
who in the slumber of my night tremors
make me think twice.

Printed in Great Britain
by Amazon

64966472R00061